The No–Bull Guide
To Acing College Life

The No-Bull Guide to Acing College Life

Dr. Andrew G. Kadar

iUniverse Star

New York Lincoln Shanghai

The No-Bull Guide to Acing College Life

iUniverse Star
an iUniverse, Inc. imprint

iUniverse books may be ordered through booksellers or by contacting:

iUniverse
2021 Pine Lake Road, Suite 100
Lincoln, NE 68512
www.iuniverse.com
1-800-Authors (1-800-288-4677)

Because of the dynamic nature of the Internet, any Web addresses or links contained in this book may have changed since publication and may no longer be valid.

The views expressed in this work are solely those of the author and do not necessarily reflect the views of the publisher, and the publisher hereby disclaims any responsibility for them.

ISBN: 978-1-60528-013-4 (pbk)
ISBN: 978-0-595-60778-5 (ebk)

Printed in the United States of America

To Kenny Kadar
and to all college freshmen.

Education is not filling a pail, but lighting a fire.

—William Butler Yeats
Irish poet (1865-1939)

The beautiful thing about learning is nobody can take it away from you.

—B.B. King
American blues musician (born 1925)

Contents

Acknowledgments

I want to thank the members of my writing group—Deborah Dahan, Bruce Gale, and Robert Hsu. They helped nurture and edit this book, as well as my other writing, for years. Thanks for your support and friendship.

I want to acknowledge the UCLA Writers' Program, and especially my dedicated and outstanding teachers—Linda Marsa, David Ulin, and Susan Vaughn.

A very special thank-you goes to Marye Anne Fox, Chancellor of the University of California, San Diego for her support.

Additional thanks to Gayle Wilson and Bobbi McKenna for their encouragement.

I also want to thank Robin Quinn and Gerald Jones for their editorial suggestions.

I want to acknowledge and thank the editors and publishing services associates of iUniverse, particularly Mike Altman and Mike Fiedler, for helping transform words on a page into this book.

I want to thank friends of Kenny Kadar from the University of Washington and from Beverly Hills High School for their feedback. And, of course, I want to thank Kenny for his many contributions to this project.

Finally, I want to thank Christine Gregory for her editorial help, encouragement, friendship, and love.

Commencement

This book contains information I wish I had before starting my freshman year.

It started out as a letter I wrote to my son…

Dear Kenny,

You already know one of the hazards of going off to college. Everybody wants to give you advice. Classmates, older friends, well-meaning relatives—even magazine articles and books—assail you with guidance. I wouldn't be surprised if Fluffy barked out some canine wisdom for you. Some of this advice is useful, but much of it consists of overblown platitudes, scare tactics, and just plain garbage.

Of course, you have to pay attention to laundry. Clean clothes will no longer appear magically in your closet. You'll have to buy your own soap and toothpaste. But I have no doubt that you will figure out such basics in short order. You won't go hungry or walk the streets of Seattle naked.

What I want to do is give you an advanced course—a few genuine pearls that can help you thrive in college and beyond. This letter contains information I wish I'd had before starting my

freshman year. So, here it is—no bull—just insights from a
coach who genuinely has your best interests at heart.

Love,

Dad

I wanted to help Kenny make a smooth transition to college,
to advise him on how to avoid some common mistakes, to share
some insights on how to flourish during the next four years. I
felt that I could have more impact with a written piece than
with a lengthy conversation. I also wanted to give Kenny something to take with him, something he could refer to later on
when I wasn't there in person. I had a lot to say, and as the writing stretched on, the letter got longer and morphed into a book.

During that process, I also started to think that my efforts
could help other college freshman as well. Kenny subsequently
shared the book with his friends, and I received positive feedback. So, I've expanded it and now offer these nuggets of
knowledge and insight to all students who are just beginning
their college years.

My qualifications for teaching this course include lots of experience—both as student and teacher.

The information that follows doesn't cover the basics of sur-
vival in college. Those everyday logistics and practicalities
belong in another text. Even without reading a book about what
to expect in daily campus life, you'll most likely manage to
remain well fed and adequately clothed at the school of your
choice.

This is the textbook for a more advanced course. *The No-Bull Guide to Acing College Life* focuses on how to ace all your classes and have a great time in the process. It guides you on the path to a truly outstanding freshman year, one that can launch you into a college experience you'll later recall with pride.

My qualifications for teaching this course include lots of experience—both as student and teacher. I earned a B.S. from the University of California at Los Angeles, and an M.D. from Yale University. I then continued my education in postdoctoral programs at the University of California at San Diego, Stanford, and Harvard. Since completing my residency, I've taught college and medical students for over twenty years. I've seen and personally experienced what works and what leads to misery during the pursuit of higher education.

Many other college orientation manuals give you detailed advice on how to overcome the everyday challenges of campus life. This one manages to be a shorter and (I believe) more useful read by focusing instead on the pursuit of excellence, the thrill of discovery, and the avoidance of a few gnarly pitfalls that can derail your plans.

It makes no pretense of providing a comprehensive guide to every situation you'll face during your freshman year. It gives you credit for having obtained a fair amount of knowledge and more than a few useful skills before arriving at this stage of your life.

My goal is to arm you with a brief, powerful manual on how to make the most of your college years.

Furthermore, I want to caution you about expecting perfection. Nobody goes through four years of college without making a few blunders. But the more bullets you can dodge, the less pain you'll suffer. (As an anesthesiologist, I am opposed to pain.)

My goal is to arm you with a brief, easy-to-digest, but powerful manual on how to make the most of your college years.

PART I

Achieving Academic Success: Ace All Your Classes

Academic success is the crucial first ingredient to a fulfilling college experience. Doing well in your studies demonstrates that you belong in college, that you can master and use complex and sophisticated information, that you deserve to occupy a space in your class. You can take justifiable pride in this accomplishment, a product of your effort and abilities. You will not only learn about the subjects you study, but also about the process of learning itself. And knowing how to learn will be a skill that you can use for the rest of your life.

When you've finished your undergraduate studies, good grades will help you advance to the next step, whether that's landing a desirable job or gaining admission to a competitive graduate program.

1

Start Strong

The beginning is the most important part of any work.

—**Plato**
Greek philosopher, 427-347 BCE

A little extra studying during the first week or two of a class will help you achieve superior results with less work overall.

Work hard from day one, and you'll be able to do well with less effort later on. A little extra studying during the first week or two of a class places you in a position to feel more comfortable with the subject, more confident in your mastery of the course material. By the end of the term, you'll achieve superior results with less work.

A hierarchy develops early in college, just as it does on sports teams and in high school classes. Everybody, students and teachers alike, can soon identify the stars, the average players, and the weak links.

Establish yourself as a strong player at the start. If you don't, you can move up in the pecking order later, but it will be far more difficult than simply maintaining your position. It's the difference between being a starter and a substitute trying to break into the lineup. As a sub, you have to perform much better than an established star to gain recognition and upgrade your standing.

College exams tend to cover far more material than their high school counterparts, making last-minute cramming more difficult and less rewarding.

Study hard to ace the first exam in each class, and the rest of the term will go a lot easier. The teaching assistants (TAs), who frequently do the grading, will expect good work from you and will often give you the benefit of the doubt. For example, if a point you're making in an essay seems unclear, a TA who knows you as a top student will be inclined to believe that you know the material, but expressed yourself less than optimally in this instance. A poorer student handing in the same text will more likely have the unclear expression attributed to a lack of knowledge. Unfair as this may be, perceptions can definitely affect your grades.

Conversely, classmates who slack off in the first few weeks will have to play catch-up. To earn a top grade, they'll have to overcome their early reputations as weak performers.

Lulled by no immediate pressure from an impending exam, many students neglect to buckle down early in a term—a major mistake. College exams tend to cover far more material than their high school counterparts, making last minute cramming more difficult and less rewarding. A strong start, regular studying from day one, will launch you on the road to success.

A powerful start is especially important during your first semester or quarter. In high school, you spent many hours in classrooms and relatively few hours studying outside of class. In college, you'll see a reversed ratio, with far fewer hours of classroom instruction and the need to study much more on your own. If you neglect to crack the books enough on your own at the start, you'll fall behind and have to work extra hard to make up for lost time. This can put you at an insurmountable disadvantage.

Starting strong in each class sets you on the path to finishing well every term.

After the first term, you'll have a better feel for what you must do to succeed. As you advance through college, you'll develop skills that will make it easier to do well with less effort. But even then, never allow yourself to become complacent during the opening days of any course and fall behind. Each new term is like a new ballgame. Previous wins boost confidence and put you in the right frame of mind, but with each new game, the scoring begins again. Put in more time studying than you think you need in the first few weeks of every course. Make that extra effort; then watch it pay off.

Points to Remember:

- Spend more time studying than you think you need during the first couple of weeks of classes.

- Establish yourself as a strong player right from the start.

- Remember, starting strong in each class sets you on the path to finishing well every term.

2

Aim High

If you think you can, you can. And if you think you can't, you're right.

—**Mary Kay Ash**
American entrepreneur, founder of
Mary Kay Cosmetics (1915-2001)

Students who don't expect to earn As rarely do.

Your goal at the start of every class should be to get an A. You might end up blowing away the competition, busting the curve, earning the highest grade in the class. But at the very least, you should *aim* for an A.

Attitude shapes results. A student who doesn't expect to earn an A rarely does.

If you come across course material that you find difficult to understand, just think about how hard it must be for your classmates who didn't start out as strongly as you did. Material that's tough for you has to be a killer for them.

Realistically, you're not likely to make every free throw, win every game, or end up with an A in every class. However, as a star player, you can certainly convert the bulk of your free throws, win the majority of your games, and get mostly As. With a winning attitude and strong effort, the odds in any class are in your favor.

Okay, so that last statement might be a stretch—but not necessarily by much. You certainly stand a better chance of earning a top grade if you aim for a top grade. Conversely, if you plan to settle for a lesser grade, you almost certainly will. So, don't sell yourself short before you find out what you can do.

Some students will definitely get As. Why not be one of them? Go for an A every time. You'll end up with a higher grade point average, greater knowledge, and a better foundation for more advanced courses.

Points to Remember:

- Your goal at the start of every class should be to earn an A.

- Students who don't expect to earn As rarely do.

- Attitude shapes results. Expect to do well.

3

Look Out for Yourself

Be alert. Your country needs more lerts.

—**Anonymous**

Even at a small college, a few hundred freshmen enroll at the same time. At large universities, they arrive by the thousands. So in either situation, you'll have plenty of competition for anything you want to do.

Many classes and programs have limited capacity. Who gets in, and who doesn't? The rules vary, particularly for honors and advanced courses. Realize that early in your college career, the preference is typically "first come, first served."

Sign up for everything you want as soon as possible, *before* you arrive on campus.

Procrastinators risk not getting their first choice of classes. That means settling for either less-desirable subjects or less-choice time slots—maybe both. Instead of the 10:00 AM course with a popular professor, you could end up in the dreaded 8:00 AM class taught by Dr. Boringhead.

The same goes for room selection in dorms. If a campus offers double and triple rooms, latecomers will end up wedged into cramped triples—in the basement, next to the bathroom, or by the trash chute.

So sign up for everything you want as soon as possible before your first term. Don't wait until you arrive on campus at the start of the year. By then, it may be too late.

Even with the best of intentions, universities cannot fully look out for each student's welfare. No school has a staff large enough to make sure that every student lives the experience that will best suit him or her. They don't have the resources to satisfy every student's preferences. You have to take the initiative to make sure that *you* get to do what you want. Take responsibility for crafting the college experience that's best for you.

Sign up as early as possible for any program that interests you. Read campus publications to find out about courses and extracurricular programs. Don't miss out on an opportunity because you learned about it too late or not at all.

Find out the rules. Read the regulations. Realize that the college administration, like any bureaucracy, has established procedures that can be frustrating, time-consuming, and even nonsensical. Ask questions. Your classmates who don't will miss out.

You are responsible for watching your own back.

Universities reserve many desirable programs for students who earn good grades. Find out about the ones offered at your school. After you demonstrate the capacity to merit top grades and become eligible for an honors program, the university will treat you better. You will receive priority in enrollment, access to facilities not open to most students, and admission to restricted courses.

Until now, your parents could run interference for you. They reminded you to sign up for classes, soccer teams, and piano lessons. They took you to the doctor to get vaccinations at the right time. They maneuvered you around obstacles placed in your path and asked questions of gatekeepers that turned an initial *no* into an ultimate *yes* (see Chapter 4).

The baton now passes into your hands. You must take over the responsibility for making sure that you don't miss out on opportunities. You can certainly handle this. You've reached a sufficient level of maturity to watch your own back. But you do have to pay attention, take initiative, and follow through.

Looking out for yourself most often comes down to being aware of what you need to do and when you need to do it. Neither your parents nor the university can look out for your best interests as well as you can. Students who don't pay attention or drag their feet lose out.

Points to Remember:

- Sign up for everything you want as early as possible, *before* you arrive on campus.

- Make the effort to learn about campus procedures and special programs.

- Watch your own back.

4

Don't Take an Easy No

You may have to fight a battle more than once to win it.

—**Margaret Thatcher**
British Prime Minister from 1979 to 1990 (born 1925)

Don't be inclined to take the first *no* as a final answer. Whenever you ask for something important, don't give in automatically or easily to authority.

If you make giving a *no* more bothersome than usual, an official may find that it's easier to say *yes* to you.

You have to be careful here because the line between admirable persistence and obnoxiousness can be slim and shady. Use sound judgment and avoid boorish behavior. Throwing a fit will more likely draw the attention of campus security than attain the results you desire. Leaving a good impression, on the other hand, can be useful in future encounters with the same official.

Just remember that the easiest answer for a bureaucrat to give (in many situations) is *no*. If you accept that as final, you permit the official who gave it to dismiss the problem you posed with minimal effort. If you resist and make that *no* more bothersome than usual, the official may find it easier to say *yes* to you and *no* to the next person. She might even admire your persistence and want to help you out. Either way, this gatekeeper changes from obstacle to ally. Sometimes asking to speak to a higher-level administrator, the first one's supervisor, can help. Ask the gatekeeper, "What can I do to get what I want?" or some appropriate variation of that question. It can start you on the road to achieving your goals.

Suppose that a class you want is full. You can give up and go away disappointed. Conversely, you can explore some preferable options:

- Will the professor allow one more highly interested student to enroll? Can you ask him or her personally?

- Is there a waiting list in case of dropouts?

- Can you audit the class, pending enrollment?

- Any chance of a new class forming in the same subject?

- Can you get advice on what you should do (perhaps from a counselor or a TA)?

By exploring all possibilities, you demonstrate motivation and perseverance in going after what you want.

Even if you don't ultimately get a *yes,* at least you'll have the satisfaction of knowing you did all you could. If you make a habit of persisting whenever the goal is important enough to warrant the effort, you can expect to turn around some, probably many, of the initial negative responses.

Points to Remember:

- Don't automatically accept *no* for an answer.

- Develop a habit of being admirably persistent in going after what you want.

- If you encounter rejection, search for alternative solutions to achieve your goal.

5

Pulverize Procrastination with The Pre-deadline Deadline

The pre-deadline deadline is the antidote to procrastination.

—Andrew G. Kadar
Author of this No-Bull Guide

Pretend that each assignment needs to be completed earlier than its actual due date.

Would you like to complete all your school work without feeling rushed or hassled? Then pay attention to this game-winning strategy. Pretend that an assignment needs to be completed earlier than its actual due date. Then finish it in time for the self-imposed, pre-deadline deadline. This strategy produces better grades with less pain—*guaranteed.*

A test on Wednesday? Tell yourself that it will be on Tuesday. Study on Monday, as if you had to be ready to take the exam the following day. Then when the inevitable happens, and the hour turns late as you pore over the books, bone-tired, but still not finished studying, you can let reality kick in. You don't have to bust your buns. You don't have to pull an exhausting all-nighter. Close your books, and sleep soundly. You have one more day. You can stop studying on Monday night, secure in the knowledge that you have only a little more to do. Then on Tuesday, you can finish the rest of your preparations for the exam easily and early. You can relax, go to bed at a decent hour, and walk confidently into the class on Wednesday—fully prepared and well rested.

You'll be way ahead of classmates who stay up late cramming on Tuesday night, still don't finish learning all the material, and then arrive to the exam exhausted and anxious. Even if they study just as many hours as you do, they end up less prepared to test well. People recall facts more easily when they feel fresh, full of energy, and confident. Furthermore, the difference between a top grade and a mediocre score often comes down to creative inspiration during the exam. For questions that require more than mere regurgitation of the textbook and lectures, you need to tap into your own resourcefulness and imagination. A creative spark has a far better chance of igniting in a well-rested and relaxed mind than in a tired and nervous one.

The same strategy works just as well for term papers. Set a pre-deadline deadline one week prior to the actual due date. Aim to complete the paper by that self-imposed time. If you then find on the pre-deadline day that you still need to double-check a point, find a reference, or rewrite a section, you can do so without strain or loss of sleep. You have another full week to finish the job.

Set a pre-deadline deadline to work smarter instead of harder.

The point is to be on top of your game. You need to avoid the helpless feeling of too little time for too much work. Eliminate unnecessary stress and distress. Prevent headaches, ulcers, sleep deprivation, and the feeling of impending doom.

By setting a pre-deadline deadline, you work smarter rather than harder. Everyone has a tendency to put off painful chores until the last minute. Then when work turns out to be more time consuming than expected (as it does on nearly all assignments), even a diligent and conscientious student can end up struggling to finish.

The pre-deadline deadline is the most effective way I know of getting work done on time. It is the *antidote to procrastination*. Remember to use it, and it will reward you every time.

I can't emphasize its value too much. Make pre-deadline deadlines part of your regular study strategy, part of your life strategy. Etch this piece of advice into your memory. It will make your life both easier and more successful.

Points to Remember:

- Tell yourself that assignment deadlines are earlier than they are—one day earlier for exams and several days earlier for papers.

- Plan your work schedule accordingly.

- Arriving well rested to an exam can mean the difference between a top grade and a mediocre one.

6

Take Advantage of Office Hours

Eighty percent of success is showing up.

—**Woody Allen**
American film maker (born 1935)

Professors make themselves available for one-on-one instruction during their office hours.

Imagine going to a rock concert, but throwing away your backstage pass and the chance to talk to the star in person. How lame would that be? Yet, students perennially do something just like that by passing up opportunities to confer with their professors outside of class.

Nearly every professor who teaches a course holds office hours, designated times when students can visit and ask questions. Even professors who lecture to classes of several hundred in large auditoriums make themselves available for one-on-one instruction. Most students neglect to take advantage of this opportunity to receive valuable guidance from a teacher they otherwise see only onstage from a distance.

Strangely, professors, even those who teach huge classes, often spend their office hours alone, without a single student coming by to make use of the time. Think of it: you possess the power to alleviate faculty loneliness and neglect! You also benefit yourself in several ways by taking advantage of office hours:

- You can ask questions to clarify concepts and gain insight into what the professor considers important. That insight will help direct your studying and may lead to a better score on the next exam or assignment.

- To the professor, you cease to exist simply as a part of the amorphous blob blankly staring back in a large lecture hall. You turn into a distinct individual, somebody who thinks about the subject and asks questions. You become a person the lecturer recognizes and respects.

- Later on, you can go to that professor for advice, and perhaps even mentoring, if you develop a special interest in his field.

TAs who hold office hours provide the same benefits. Seize the opportunity to spend additional time learning from them.

Don't go for an office visit purely for the sake of going, but definitely do so whenever you have any questions about the material. Take advantage of the best source of answers—your teachers.

Getting to know a professor personally can help when you need a recommendation.

Perhaps students shy away from office hours out of a misguided fear that they will appear ignorant or foolish in front of their instructors. Forget it. Nobody expects you to know everything about the subject; you wouldn't need to take the class if you were an expert in the field. You can also help the professor become a more effective teacher by providing information about what material needs to be clarified and amplified in subsequent lectures. It's a rare professor who will repay you by making you feel foolish. Far more likely, the teacher will reward you with encouragement and extra information to help you understand the material and ace the next exam.

Getting to know a professor personally can also help when you apply to graduate school or for a job. A student who demonstrates interest by asking thoughtful questions has a far better prospect of receiving a strong recommendation than one who merely occupies a seat in class.

Going to office hours takes little effort and provides a bounty of benefits. Now that you know this, don't forget it. Upperclassmen and graduate students work for years to earn the prerequisites for admission to advanced courses that boast small student-teacher ratios. You can receive similar instruction and even the benefit of a one-on-one tutorial just by walking through an open door and expressing some curiosity about the subject. Be among the smart few who take advantage of this opportunity.

Points to Remember:

- Nearly all professors keep regular office hours for individual consultation.

- Talking with your professor directly can help you to better understand the subject matter.

- Becoming an individual in the eyes of your professor can later lead to valuable recommendations.

7

Lighten Your Load: Choosing Your First Class Schedule

Fools rush in where angels fear to tread.

—**Alexander Pope**
English poet (1688-1744)

The challenges of starting college demand as much effort as a hard academic class.

The transition from high school to college is complex and difficult. Dealing with all the new challenges and responsibilities you will confront demands as much effort and time as a rigorous academic course. Therefore, I recommend that you take one less class in your course load during your first quarter than you will in subsequent quarters.

Don't mistake this suggestion for advice to slack off. Recognize instead that learning to be a college student requires significant effort.

You have to learn to learn on your own.

I know that you feel ready for college, and you certainly are (especially after you combine the information in this book with what you already know). Nevertheless, to thrive as a college student, you'll have to adapt to numerous significant changes in your life—not an easy assignment for anybody. You'll need to:

- *Adjust to a markedly different daily schedule:*
  Compared to your high school experience, a much greater portion of your studying will take place outside the classroom. You'll spend more time with books and instructional media, less with teachers. Having to spend fewer hours inside classrooms will provide you with greater freedom to allocate your time. But you also assume the responsibility of putting the hours of each day to good use. Students who fail to appreciate this can suffer dire consequences. Having fewer class hours doesn't mean more time to goof off. You have to learn to learn on your own.

- *Settle into a different pace:*
  Since college courses cover a greater volume of material and require more work than their high school counterparts, you'll need to move faster and develop greater efficiency in your study habits.

- *Deal with a higher level of competition:*
  Many of your classmates will be more mature and ambitious than your high school classmates. Particularly if you're at a school with highly selective admissions, it's likely your fellow freshmen were all stars in their prior schools. You'll

need to elevate your game up a notch to compete at this new level.

- *Acclimate to new living arrangements:*
  All your stuff must fit into a fraction of a dorm room. You have to learn to get along with roommates, people who won't go away when you get tired of their company.

- *Familiarize yourself with a new town:*
  You'll have to find out where to buy pens, CDs, underwear, and movie tickets. You'll need to learn about your new surroundings so you can make necessary purchases and enjoy recreational activities.

All of these adjustments take time and energy. How much? They require at least the equivalent effort that should go into one hard academic class. Remember that when choosing your first course schedule. Think of it as enrolling in *College Life 101*. Three classes, along with this unrecorded one, will feel like four.

Enrolling in fewer classes will improve your chances of doing well in all of your classes.

By taking a lighter official schedule, you'll be less likely to feel overwhelmed by the combination of academic requirements and life adjustments. Enrolling in fewer classes will enable you to study more thoroughly for each course and will improve your chances of doing well in all of them. Once you've learned to cope—actually to shine—you'll be able to take an extra class to make up for the fewer units during your first term. It'll be a lot easier to take an additional class the following year than tackling a full load right at the start.

Alternatively, you can register for the standard number of units, so long as two of your courses are known to be ones that require less work. Campus jargon for these classes varies from school to school. Over time, you may hear references to *gut* courses, *joke* classes, or *micks*—after Mickey Mouse. Individual soft courses may have their very own nicknames. An easy geology class might be known as "Rocks for Jocks."

Whether you actually take one less course or double up on easy ones, give yourself a break in the first semester. You'll enjoy life more, and you'll position yourself to earn better grades in all your classes.

Points to Remember:

- Learning to be a college student takes as much time and effort as a difficult academic class.

- During your first term, take one less course or two easier courses to compensate.

8

Picking a Major:
When and Why

When you come to a fork in the road, take it.

—**Yogi Berra**
American baseball player/manager (born 1925)

Choosing a major gives you a home base and counselors who'll look after you.

The university doesn't have a Department of Indecision. You can't earn a B.S. (Bachelor of Science degree) in indecision, even if you become a master at it. And just to *p*ile it *h*igher and *d*eeper, no university grants PhDs in this subject either.

Picking a major gives you direction and a home base. It allows you to plan a schedule of required and elective classes that lead to a specific degree. It also provides you with counselors who'll look after you more closely than the administrators who loosely guide the lost souls wandering in the limbo of indecision.

"What do I want to do for the rest of my life?" **may be the wrong question.**

If you find one discipline you're most passionate about, your choice of major will become easy. But even if you don't, you still need to make a decision. Think of it as a fork in the road. You can angle left or right safely. However, if you continue straight ahead, you'll drive off the road and crash into a tree. Taking either branch of the fork will produce better results than not making up your mind. By choosing a major, you stay on the path to a worthwhile destination.

If you have trouble deciding on a major, perhaps you're asking yourself the wrong question, or maybe just too big a question. *"What do I want to do for the rest of my life?"* can sound overwhelming. The whole concept of "the rest of your life" might freak you out. You may not be able to decide on any single field for that long. So, choose one to study for only a few years.

You can change your major if you subsequently find another field that excites you more.

A major doesn't commit you for life to a particular field. You can change your mind later on. During my years of higher education, I went from physics to biomedical engineering to medicine to surgery to anesthesiology. As you can see, it can take several steps to get to no pain (the goal of anesthesiology). If your first choice of major doesn't continue to excite you, you retain the option of switching to something different at a later date. By fulfilling the requirements of any major, you demonstrate the capacity to perform at a level that will get you admitted to graduate or professional school in other fields as well. Many students earn a bachelors degree in one discipline and attend graduate school in another. As for employment opportunities, graduating from college with any major makes you eligible for many jobs that require a college degree.

Pick a major by the end of your freshman year.

You can continue to take classes in subjects outside your major throughout all of your college years. Along the way, you may discover another field that you like even more. If that happens, you can choose to change your major, or perhaps just switch to a new discipline after graduation. Your initial choice is not set in stone.

Many universities allow students to postpone declaring a major for two years. Some people advise taking advantage of that entire time, unless you're certain about your choice. I disagree.

The longer you wait to declare a major, the longer you miss out on all the aforementioned advantages of having a set course of study. You may even need to take an extra year to graduate if you don't begin enrolling in required courses early enough. Don't risk putting yourself in that situation.

Take the plunge: declare a major by the end of your freshman year.

Points to Remember:

• Make a commitment to yourself to decide on a major by the end of your freshman year.

- Choosing any major is better than having no major.

- You can change your major later on if you discover another field more to your liking.

PART II

Staying Alive: Getting to Graduation with All Body Parts Intact

Academic success is terrific, but you also need to survive to graduation day in good health. This section will cover the basics of staying alive by coaching you on how to avoid some potentially serious problems—obesity, eating disorders, pregnancy, and permanent body alterations. It also includes a no-bull tutorial on alcohol and drugs. I'll try to keep the gory details to just the essentials, while still providing you with adequate knowledge about these complex and sometimes controversial subjects.

As you read this material, please understand that I am not preaching from the viewpoint of a concerned parent (although I am one). In this section, I'm writing as a medical doctor and educator. My goal is to provide you with scientific information to help you make informed and wise decisions that will safeguard your health.

Of course, for any questions about your health, you need to consult a doctor who knows you. The information in this book should not be considered a substitute for advice from a physician. For legal protection, I need to expressly disclaim responsibility for any adverse effects arising from the use of information contained in this book.

9

Propersize: Eat Well And Avoid the Dreaded "Freshman 15"

Food is an important part of a balanced diet.

—**Fran Lebowitz**
American author/humorist (born 1951)

The dreaded "freshman 15" strikes fear in the hearts of those at risk.

If you haven't heard about it yet, you will soon: the dreaded "freshman 15," the number of pounds first-year college students supposedly gain on average. The prospect strikes fear—even horror—in the hearts of those at risk.

The actual situation is not as bad as advertised.

All-you-can-eat dining, large portions, high-calorie snacks from vending machines, social munching, stress-eating, beer binges at parties, and late-night fast-food runs can all add up to more calories than anybody can possibly use. Combine these ingredients with diminished exercise, and you have a recipe for super-sizing your body.

The actual situation, however, is not as bad as advertised. Several studies examining freshman weight gain put the number far below the legendary 15 pounds. For example, researchers from Tufts University reported a median weight increase of 4.5 pounds for women and 6 pounds for men. Another study at the University of Alabama at Tuscaloosa found a 4-pound weight gain among its women and no gain among its men.

Of course, some students do manage to overachieve in caloric consumption and balloon up even beyond the infamous 15. With a little knowledge and some prudent precautions, you can avoid joining their ranks.

To start you on that quest for knowledge, I will now present Dr. Kadar's ultra-simple synopsis of life-transforming diet formulas. Eating patterns "guaranteed" to improve your health come in three basic flavors: low-fat diets, low-carbohydrate diets, and magic-ingredient diets. Here, in brief, are the salient elements of each:

- *Low-fat diets*

   Traditional programs promoted by the U.S. Department of Health and Human Services, the Department of Agriculture, and the American Heart Association emphasize limiting the amount of fat in your diet. The Pritikin and Ornish programs prescribe even more severe fat restrictions.

The fundamental problem with the low-fat approach is that it hasn't worked.

Restricting fat intake makes intuitive sense. Fat is calorie-dense. One gram of it—around one-fourteenth of a tablespoon of butter—contains nine calories. An equal amount of carbohydrates or protein (by weight) has only four. So, for any given weight of food, reducing the fat content automatically decreases the number of calories.

The fundamental problem with the low-fat approach is that it hasn't worked. While the portion of calories derived from fat in the average American diet has declined from around 45 percent to 34 percent since 1965, the incidence of obesity has gone up. Why? Because fat satisfies hunger. If you limit fat intake, you tend to eat more to feel full. The added calories in the extra food add pounds.

To maintain or reduce weight, a low-fat diet needs to be coupled with calorie restriction. But a diet that limits both fat and calories can cause hunger. If you then satisfy this hunger by binging, the excess calorie consumption will cause you to gain weight.

• *Low-carbohydrate diets*

By restricting carbohydrate consumption, Atkins postulated that your body will absorb and retain less fat.

The late Dr. Robert Atkins promoted the most popular version of the carbohydrate-restricted diets. The Zone and the South Beach Diet are more recent popular entries in this category.

Carbohydrates include sugars (such as table sugar and hard candy) and starches (such as rice and potatoes). Eating carbohydrates raises the level of insulin in blood.

That, in turn, causes increased absorption and retention of fat. By restricting carbohydrate consumption, Atkins postulated that your body will absorb and retain less fat. So while it restricts the eating of carbohydrates, his diet allows you to gorge yourself on as much fat and protein as you like.

This diet has an obvious appeal to meat lovers. Devour the steak; hold the potatoes. Wolf down hamburgers and hot dogs; cut out the buns. Over time however, people do seem to miss the potatoes, pasta, and bread. The National Weight Control Registry, which tracks people who have lost at least 30 pounds and have kept it off for over a year, lists almost no Atkins dieters.

This eating pattern can also cause a number of health problems, including kidney stones and diminished kidney function, osteoporosis, colon cancer, and possibly heart disease. One study, published in the New England Journal of Medicine in 2003 and the Annals of Internal Medicine in 2004, caused a sensation by reporting favorable cholesterol and triglyceride changes after low-carbohydrate dieting for six months and for one year. This raised the possibility that the Atkins diet could actually decrease the risk of heart disease, at least in the short-run. The long-term cardiac effects of a low-carbohydrate, high-fat diet, however, remain unknown. Less life-threatening, but not so ideal in social situations, the Atkins diet will also give you a mean case of bad breath.

• *Magic-ingredient diets*

The real secret of single-food diets turns out to be nothing more than calorie restriction.

Some people have come out with diets centered around a special ingredient that they claim can mysteriously and miraculously produce weight loss. Whether it's the cabbage-soup, the grapefruit, or any other single-food diet, their real secret turns out to be nothing more than calorie restriction. By limiting the amount of all foods, except for the magic ingredient, these regimens reduce calorie consumption. After a few days, a dieter might get nauseated just thinking about another bowl of cabbage soup. The nausea, augmented by boredom, limits eating and produces weight loss. Unfortunately, such a diet also results in hunger and malnutrition.

Consequently, these magic-food diets are temporary measures that ultimately produce the yo-yo effect of alternating weight loss and gain. Dieters first lose weight while starving themselves. They later regain all their lost pounds—and often many times more—by binging to satisfy pent-up hunger once going off the regimen. Obviously, this is a most unhealthy sequence of events and should be avoided.

Some students may seek to control their weight by taking any one of a variety of pharmacologic agents, such as diet pills and supplements. Most of these so-called aids are useless and reduce only the weight of your wallet. Others contain potent chemicals that have serious side effects, including heart rhythm disturbances, kidney failure, and death. Don't be misled by claims that a diet aid is "all-natural" or used by enchanting beauties in some exotic corner of the world. All the compounds that actually enhance weight loss are dangerous and should be avoided. (The one exception to this rule applies only to the very small segment of students who suffer from severe obesity and may benefit from a physician-supervised regimen that does include prescription medication.)

Anorexia (self-starvation) and bulimia (forced vomiting after eating) are even more dangerous strategies for weight control. If you engage in these highly risky and often fatal practices, seek medical help today. It may save your life.

So, what should you do? First of all, don't swallow every bit of advice you get about healthy eating. You're bound to end up with a big fat headache and bad case of indigestion.

Ever hear the story of the blind men who examined an elephant? The guy who touched the side of the elephant decided that the animal resembled a wall; the one who came up to an ear said it was like a fan; the man who touched a leg concluded that the creature must be a type of tree; the examiner of the tail decided that the animal was rope-like; and the man who felt a tusk declared that the elephant had a body similar to a spear. Like good experimental scientists, each man investigated a specific part of the beast and made a valid observation. Then, unlike good scientists, but very much like the purveyors of diet and nutrition hyperbole, each blind examiner extrapolated from a small bit of valid data to reach an overly broad, and therefore wrong conclusion. Please recall this cautionary tale the next time you hear about a new, super-wonderful, "scientifically proven" diet.

Like the elephant, human diet is a highly complex subject. Despite numerous studies and many thousands of accurate observations by battalions of highly trained researchers world-wide, our view of nutrition remains incomplete and hazy.

A multitude of variables, ranging from heredity to numerous environmental factors, complicate the situation. Bona fide results from a study on a set of people in one place may not hold up in other groups. More specifically, they may not apply to you. Gender, race, age, location, weather, exercise, illness, stress, and other factors too numerous to list may all modify the data. To complicate matters even further, variations in individual body chemistry can make your response to a set of nutrients different from the average, even for your age and sex.

None of this information has stopped a whole lot of people from coming up with gospel-like pronouncements on what we should all be eating. So, *caveat emptor*—buyer beware. When it comes to diet prescriptions, ingest at your peril.

What diet advice has stood the test of time? Eat more fruits and vegetables.

Hucksters tend to stick by their dietary formulas, even when research produces contradicting data. More responsible sources incorporate new information into their recommendations over time. Therefore in April 2005, the U.S. Department of Agriculture updated its familiar 1992 Food Guide Pyramid. The new MyPyramid emphasizes the importance of exercise in healthy weight management by showing a cartoon character jogging up steps on one side of the pyramid. You can find more information on the current USDA guidelines, along with personalized recommendations, by logging on to MyPyramid.gov.

So, what exactly do food scientists know about nutrition and diet that has stood the test of time? People should eat more fruits and vegetables, because they contain vital nutrients and are not calorie-dense. They will fill your belly and satisfy your hunger without packing excess weight onto your body. You can eat everything else you want in moderation.

Avoid binging. No multiple trips to that all-you-can-eat cafeteria line. Choose an apple or a pear over chips or cookies for a snack. Use common sense.

To dodge the "freshman 15," you also need to stay physically active. Some students who played on their high school soccer or softball teams shy away from sports in college. If you eat the same amount of food you ate last year, but exercise less, you will absolutely, positively gain weight. To prevent this, join an intramural team, hit the gym, or run up the side of a pyramid (or any other set of stairs if pyramids are scarce on your campus).

Vigorous exercise, several times per week, will make you both look and feel better. If you start seeing weight gain, nip it in the bud with fruits, vegetables, and exercise.

Points to Remember:

- Pay attention to your eating habits to avoid weight gain during your freshman year.

- There is no such thing as a "scientifically-proven," perfect diet.

- Eating more fruits and vegetables and exercising regularly provide the only time-proven strategy for better health and weight control.

- One piece of valid data can't be extrapolated to accurately describe either an elephant or what you should eat.

10

Get the Straight Dope On Magical Mystery Drugs

We drink to one another's health and spoil our own.

—**Jerome K. Jerome**
English author (1859-1927)

Alcohol and drugs are a fact of life on college campuses. Since this is a no-bull guide, what you're about to read will neither exaggerate nor ignore the dangers and pleasures of intoxication. I'm not offering judgments, just the straight dope about the effects of alcohol and drugs (with special focus on marijuana, cocaine, Adderall, and ecstasy).

The danger from alcohol depends on quantity.

Alcohol is by far the most commonly ingested mind-altering substance on and off campus. If you're too young to drink legally in your state, you do risk getting busted. Enforcement of underage alcohol consumption laws can be lax, but presidential daughters, famous actors, and many other underage drinkers learned their sobering lessons the hard way.

Beyond that, most people can drink safely *in moderation*. Chances are you've already downed a bottle of beer, a glass of wine, or a cocktail without suffering any ill effects.

The faster you drink alcohol, the greater the risk of reaching a dangerous level of intoxication.

The danger comes from quantity. A large amount of alcohol can make you sick; a really large amount can make you really, really sick; an even greater amount can kill you.

The faster you consume alcohol, the less chance your body has to process it—hence, the greater the risk of reaching a dangerous level of intoxication. Beware of chugalug games and contests. Don't get trapped in situations where you're coerced to drink large amounts of alcohol rapidly. That's how fraternity pledges, compelled to pour down copious volumes of liquor during initiation hazing, sometimes die.

A small amount of alcohol—the amount in a single drink, maybe two—causes a relaxing effect that most people find pleasant. Larger quantities produce nausea, vomiting, dizziness, excessive sweating, loss of coordination, and blurry vision. By the time you're falling-down drunk and vomiting, you won't impress anyone with your sophistication. When drinking beyond this point, you risk shock, convulsions, coma, and ultimately death.

So, nurse your drink and consume it over a half hour or more. Give the alcohol time to act. Monitor how it affects you. Don't lose control. Try to avoid puking on your date or any of your friends.

If you get a hangover, take an aspirin or a Tylenol, and drink plenty of fluids. No, no—not alcoholic fluids. Drink plain water; dehydration is a major cause of hangovers. You might even be able to prevent a hangover by drinking plenty of nonalcoholic beverages along with your booze.

Alcohol causes both immediate and long-term health problems.

Alcohol-induced loss of judgment can lead to fatally poor decisions such as driving after drinking or getting into a car with a drunk driver. When sober, you know better than that.

Alcohol is a sedative. It may augment the effects of medicines such as sleeping pills and tranquilizers. The combination of pills and alcohol can lead to a serious overdose, even a coma. Alcohol can alter the absorption and effects of other medicines as well. So, if you take medication, be extra careful. Ask your doctor about the interaction of alcohol with your prescription medicines.

Chronic alcohol excess can lead to a variety of health problems, particularly liver injury. Some students do become alcoholics and suffer the humiliating and health-destroying effects of that affliction. If you indulge when you should be studying, your grades will suffer, and academic failure may put a premature end to your college drinking days. Before that happens, seek help. You can begin to assess whether you have an alcohol problem with a short questionnaire such as the Michigan

Alcohol Screening Test (MAST), which is readily available over the Internet.

Alcohol packs lots of calories. Drinking can make you fat.

If you're concerned about your physique, you should be aware that alcoholic beverages are not calorie free. A 12-ounce bottle of beer packs about 145 calories; a 4-ounce glass of Merlot has 95; and a 3-ounce Margarita contains around 170 calories. Compare those numbers to a McDonald's Quarter Pounder, which checks in at 420 calories. So, sipping a few cocktails could add more calories to your diet than eating a moderate-sized meal. Alcohol consumption can result in unwanted campus prominence—in the shape of a protruding beer belly.

Alcoholic beverages can also serve as stealth delivery vehicles for drugs you don't intend to take. Rohypnol, better known as "roofies" or the "date rape drug," is the brand name for flunitrazepam, a tranquilizer chemically similar to Valium, but more powerful. It produces sleepiness and amnesia. Unscrupulous predators can spike a drink with Rohypnol to facilitate a sexual assault on an incapacitated victim, who afterwards might not even remember what happened.

The bottom line on alcohol: monitor your intake, and remember the risks.

Marijuana, the most common of illicit drugs, is not legal anywhere in the United States. Sobering visits from your local police department therefore present an added level of risk beyond any health concerns.

For most occasional smokers, marijuana doesn't cause any significant physical harm. Users frequently experience the giggles, the munchies, and red eyes. Silly laughter can make a person appear stupid, and increased appetite can lead to dreaded weight gain. Red eyes may scare small children, but will produce no permanent damage. A rapid heart rate, also common, poses no danger to a young person with a healthy heart. Loss of coordination, however, does make driving dangerous. Sometimes, it makes even standing up and walking dangerous.

Some people do experience anxiety, paranoia, and hallucinations with marijuana. Those who begin with mild emotional problems can trigger a worsening of their symptoms. So-called "bad trips" can lead to further, sometimes debilitating, psychological problems.

Chronic smoking of marijuana can lead to lung damage similar to injury from cigarettes.

Of course, frequent marijuana smoking that interferes with fulfilling other life responsibilities differs markedly from casual use. Think of the contrast between an alcoholic and someone who drinks an occasional beer.

Chronic use of marijuana can lead to lung damage similar to that caused by cigarette smoking. Since marijuana tends to be inhaled more deeply than tobacco, each joint causes far more damage than a single cigarette.

Marijuana can also be blended into foods, such as the legendary Alice B. Toklas brownies. These culinary delights present an additional danger because of the delay between the time of ingestion and the onset of effects. Smokers can stop taking tokes when they reach a desired high and will get no higher. But when someone who ate a marijuana-laced dessert reaches a desired high, he can't turn off the continuing absorption of additional cannabis already in his intestines, but not yet taken up by the bloodstream. This uncontrolled additional uptake can easily lead to higher-than-expected doses and more unpleasant side effects.

Many other drugs are far more dangerous than either alcohol or marijuana. Even a cursory discussion of all the ones misused and abused would expand this book to a length far greater than you want to read or I want to write. So, I'll confine the rest of this discussion to three of the most commonly abused central nervous system stimulants—cocaine, Adderall, and ecstasy.

Cocaine comes from the leaves of coca, a plant indigenous to the Andes Mountains region of South America. Natives of Peru and Bolivia chew coca leaves to relive fatigue. The white powder commonly snorted in the United States contains a far greater concentration of cocaine than found in the plant. The powder can be easily converted to the crystalline form, called "crack" or "rock," which is then smoked.

Cocaine causes more hospital visits and deaths than any other illicit drug.

Cocaine stimulates the cardiovascular and nervous systems, leading to a broad range of adverse consequences. It produces arterial constriction, which leads to higher blood pressure. Anxiety, agitation, and paranoia can be troublesome. In severe cases, these psychological problems will result in hospitalization. Heart attacks, strokes, and seizures account for most emergency room visits and deaths. Cocaine causes more hospital admissions and deaths than any other illicit drug. According to data compiled for the United States Department of Health and Human Services, emergency department visits due to cocaine abuse outnumber those involving marijuana by around 60 percent, heroin by 160 percent, and stimulants, including amphetamines, by 200 percent.

Adderall is a prescription drug commonly used to treat attention deficit disorder and attention deficit hyperactivity disorder in school-aged children. Because so many kids receive prescriptions for this medicine, young people possess lots of Adderall tablets and capsules. Ease of access therefore contributes to the potential for abuse.

Amphetamines can cause cardiac problems by raising heart rate and blood pressure.

The chemical composition of Adderall consists of a combination of amphetamine and a related compound called dextroamphetamine. These two agents act on the brain by increasing the levels of two other chemicals, dopamine and norepinephrine—which in turn can boost attention span and wakefulness. The appeal of this effect to a student who wants to pull an all-nighter or just study longer for an exam is self-evident.

So, what's the downside? Amphetamines cause both immediate and cumulative health hazards.

For one thing, they can produce cardiac problems by rais-
ing heart rate and blood pressure. You've probably heard of
college athletes dying during rigorous football or basketball
drills. The cause is often either a heart rhythm irregularity or
very high temperature induced by a combination of exercise
and amphetamine or a related drug.

Amphetamines wire you, making it difficult to sleep after you
finish studying and want to get some rest. By interfering with
your biological clock, they can cause you to crash and be sleepy
just in time for the exam. Sometimes students take a second
dose of the drug to counteract the comedown from the first, but
taking more at this point can lead to restlessness, fidgeting, and
tremors that diminish the ability to sit still and concentrate on
the subject at hand. Other side effects include headache, dizziness, a dry mouth, and gastrointestinal disturbances (stomach
ache, nausea, vomiting, and both diarrhea and constipation—a
heck of a combination). Amphetamines can also trigger hallucinations, manic symptoms, paranoia, and psychosis.

Chronic amphetamine use induces changes in body chemistry, forcing the body to crave ever-larger doses to achieve the
same effect. Doctors monitor ADHD patients for this development, called tolerance, and use it as a signal to change treatment, either to a higher dose or to a different therapy. Chronic
use can also lead to depression and suicide. So can abrupt
withdrawal. Students experimenting on themselves with
Adderall may not be aware of these reactions or know how to
deal with them, and could suffer the consequences.

A drug that promises to help you study longer can be seductive. It may seem safe because it's prescribed to so many of your classmates or their younger siblings. But the brain chemistry of someone with ADHD is abnormal. If you have normal brain function, Adderall is wrong for you. Furthermore, this drug can cause problems even for the most closely monitored ADHD patients. Self-prescribing it poses unnecessary risks. You may feel lucky, confident that you won't suffer any adverse reactions, but so do all the students who end up in emergency rooms and psychiatric wards.

Better to mind the pre-deadline deadline and avoid the need or the temptation to experiment with this hazardous study aid.

Ecstasy causes long-term brain damage, diminishing memory and thinking capacity.

Ecstasy is another amphetamine compound, but it's purely recreational and far more dangerous. Its chemical name is *methylenedioxymethamphetamine* or MDMA. It can lead to anxiety and paranoia, as well as fever, chills, excessive sweating, and dehydration. Most ominously, it can cause a racing heart and irregular rhythms. Heart rhythm disturbances and dehydration account for most deaths from this "party drug."

If you're lucky and don't suffer immediate catastrophic effects, the drug ecstasy will cause long-term damage to your brain, diminishing your memory and thinking capacity. Diagnostic scans of repeat ecstasy users reveal structural damage to nerve cells in the brain. Can you think of anything dumber than voluntarily taking a substance that's guaranteed to make you dumber by chemically drilling little sponge-holes in your brain?

If you're handed a tablet or capsule at a party, you have no way of knowing what's in it.

Another major problem with the drug ecstasy is, "You never know what you're gonna get." Think of staring at a box of poisoned chocolates. The chemical composition of more than half the stuff that passes for ecstasy is actually *methamphetamine,* the drug more commonly known on the street as *speed.* Like ecstasy, speed is an amphetamine derivative and a cause of deadly heart rhythm irregularities.

If you're handed a tablet or capsule at a party, you have no way of knowing what's in it or how much. Ecstasy is a back-alley, illegal brew made in unregulated labs with no quality control. It's mixed in bathtubs, sinks, and other containers potentially laced with just about anything. Brain damage symptoms reported from the use of drugs sold as ecstasy include tremors and rigidity similar to that caused by the neurological disorder, Parkinson's Syndrome. As a result of sloppy mixing, the amount of active ingredients can vary widely from one pill to the next. Two people taking identical-looking tablets from the same source could be ingesting widely different amounts of whatever the active ingredients happen to be. This is true not only of stuff passing as ecstasy, but also of mind-altering party pills sold as anything else.

A large variety of other stimulants, sedatives, narcotics, and anesthetics can deliver agony similar to the drug ecstasy. I don't plan to go through their profiles one by one. This section probably already contains more gory details than you expected, but in order to thrive in college, you do need to survive. Knowing the risks drugs pose should help you make smarter decisions that will keep you away from harm and regret.

Consider one additional caveat—taking a combination of drugs or drugs and alcohol can produce especially dangerous consequences. The toxicity of one substance can magnify the toxicity of the other, making the total risk greater than the sum of its parts. For example, the incidence of sudden death from the combined intake of cocaine and alcohol is more than twenty times as great as from cocaine alone.

So be careful with drugs and alcohol. Don't take any pills or capsules for recreation. Don't gamble your health and life on a mystery drug!

Points to Remember:

- Alcohol and marijuana pose no major health risks in moderation, but be aware of the dangers of higher doses, chronic use, and the legal pitfalls.

- Cocaine causes heart attacks, strokes, and seizures.

- Amphetamines and all other recreational drugs pose both immediate and long-term health hazards, including permanent brain damage and death.

- Don't trust that you know what you're getting when offered an illicit drug.

- Never gamble with your life by taking a mystery drug.

11

Avoid Permanent Scars: Tawdry Tales of Tattoos and Piercings

Beauty is only skin deep, and the world is full of thin-skinned people.

—**Richard Armour**
American poet/humorist (1906-1989)

Sooner or later, many tattooed folks regret their decision to be marked.

Do you remember sitting in front of the TV and singing along with a certain purple dinosaur? Did you used to admire the Power Rangers? Think back to all the things you once considered cool, but now regard as infantile or just plain stupid. Imagine having a Barney or Power Ranger tattoo decorating your arm or your butt. Do you relish the prospect of being branded permanently with tastes from an earlier time in your life? How would you feel about having to wear an image you no longer like?

The number one problem with tattoos and most body piercings is that they stay with you forever. Unlike an item of clothing, they cannot be discarded easily. You can't give an old tattoo away to charity or dump it in the trash. It goes under your skin and becomes part of your body—not for as long as you want it, but for as long as you live.

Time cures even the worst haircut or dye job, but old tattoos just get uglier as they age. With the passage of time, the ink seeps out over a wider area, making the image look faded and smeared. As your body changes, so will the artwork covering it. Slender young dancing girls on forearms develop middle-age spread as the arms' owners put on weight. Butterfly wings become asymmetrical, and all sorts of geometric shapes get distorted to mush. You can just imagine the sad fate of pictures injected into thighs and butts.

Tattooing and piercing can put your health in jeopardy.

If you can count on making a living as a professional musician or an NBA player, a tattoo won't retard your career. But since the odds of becoming a star in these fields barely exceed those of winning the lottery, you might want to have a plan B. In a lot of other environments, only lower-echelon and less educated workers display body alterations. Be aware that many people have a negative opinion of tattoos. Do you want to show up for a job interview or for work with an indelible sign labeling you a loser? Certainly not everyone thinks of tattoos that way, but some of your colleagues and bosses will. Incidentally, so will many prospective dates and mates. Don't put yourself at this unnecessary disadvantage.

Tattooing also jeopardizes your health. Repeated needle sticks hurt. If you enjoy being jabbed by needles over and over again, you'll love the experience of getting a tattoo. Of course, you should expect to bleed after all that needling. The trauma may cause scarring and keloid formation. Injected pigments sometimes induce an allergic reaction. Bacterial infection can produce additional suffering, including fever, pain, inflammation, and pus oozing from the site. Any equipment that comes in contact with blood, unless properly sterilized, can infect subsequent subjects with hepatitis and the human immunodeficiency virus (HIV).

Legions of tattooed folks sooner or later regret their decision to be marked. As I noted earlier, your tastes will change over time. While remorse is common, no matter what the image, inking the name of a lover under the skin probably presents the highest risk of subsequent intense regret. If the lover departs, the indelible reminder endures long past the romance. I once treated a woman who had "This way Jose" tattooed in cursive letters just under her navel. A red arrow below the writing pointed straight down to her pubis. Jose had apparently lost his way for good, and she wanted the directions removed.

There are some options for tattoo removal. Unwanted images can be cut out, sanded away or bombarded with laser impulses. The best choice depends on the size of the tattoo, the depth of placement of the ink, and the chemicals in the dyes. All of these procedures usually leave visible scars and cause both physical and financial pain.

Excision works best on small images. After the tattoo is cut out, the remaining skin edges have to be brought together and sutured closed. For larger images, excision must be performed in stages or covered with a skin graft, which leaves a larger and more prominent scar.

Sanding, usually with a rotary abrasive instrument, works best on ink positioned in the more superficial strata of skin. With deeper tattoos, more layers of cells need to be peeled away before any dye can be removed. Bleeding, scarring, and skin discoloration can complicate this procedure.

Laser works by breaking up ink into small fragments that the body's immune system can remove. The effectiveness of laser treatments depends on the chemical composition and the depth in skin of the targeted dyes. Most tattoos require multiple treatments, usually from four to ten, each costing several hundred dollars. The end result can be compromised by scarring and skin discoloration. With any technique, getting rid of an unwanted image is a far more complicated and costly procedure than the initial tattooing.

Piercing also involves breaking the skin and can induce all the problems associated with that violation: redness and swelling, infection, bleeding, large scars, keloids, and tears. These problems occur more frequently than you might think. A survey of pierced college students in 2001, conducted by researchers from Pace University and the United States Olympic Committee, found an overall incidence of medical complications (from bacterial infections, bleeding, and local trauma) of 17 percent. Other studies have reported rates of greater than 10 percent each of infection, redness and swelling, drainage, and crusting. Even uncomplicated piercings take one to twelve months to heal. If you've had your ears pierced and wore studs to keep the holes open, this should come as no surprise.

In addition, each part of the body can suffer its own unique set of problems when pierced. All of the following complications have been reported in medical journals.

Jewelry inserted into tongues and lips can chip and crack teeth. The 2001 survey reported a nearly 10 percent incidence of oral and dental injuries in college students with pierced tongues. Tongue piercings can also produce speech problems, including a lisp. Oral infection and swelling can bring about an airway obstruction severe enough to require the placement of a breathing tube in the trachea and necessitate mechanical ventilation for several days.

Navel piercing can result in months of troublesome oozing and crusting. More ominously, some people have come down with bacterial endocarditis, a heart infection, following this procedure.

Nipple piercing can cause an abscess, a collection of pus inside the breast. This painful condition requires treatment with surgical drainage and antibiotics. It can also cause scarring and decreased sensitivity.

Penile pricking can impede the flow and aim of the urinary stream, causing some men to have to sit to urinate. One study reported a 39 percent incidence of problematic urinary flow changes. Both male and female genital piercings can also result in site tenderness and decreased sexual sensitivity. Genital jewelry can tear condoms, increasing the risk of sexually transmitted diseases and unwanted pregnancy.

The female partner of a man with a penile piercing can also suffer adversity. One case report described a woman whose partner lost a metallic bead from his penile ring during sexual activity. She went to her local hospital, anxiously seeking help in retrieving the lost jewelry from inside her vagina. When manual and speculum examinations failed to locate the elusive bead, her doctor ordered an X-ray. The film revealed the missing ornament over the left side of her pelvis, but its exact location remained unclear. Further questioning revealed that the couple had engaged in oral sex just prior to vaginal intercourse. The woman had apparently swallowed the bead, which showed up on the X-ray inside her intestine. She passed the bead rectally within a week.

Points to Remember:

- Tastes change over time. Unhappiness with an old tattoo is very common.

- A significant percentage of piercings result in health problems.

- Don't set yourself up for regret. Avoid permanent body alterations!

12

Take Charge of Contraception

A fast word about oral contraception. I asked a girl to go to bed with me and she said "no."

—**Woody Allen**
(his second act in this book, see Chapter 6)

Preventing unwanted pregnancy is a joint responsibility.

An unplanned pregnancy can derail not only your college education, but also your plans for life. Of course, abstinence is the surest way to prevent pregnancy. If you choose not to go that route, you need to exercise proper precautions to avoid disaster. You've heard that it takes two to tango. It also takes two to mess up contraception. In other words, you both have to screw up at the same time. If you each take responsibility for preventing an unwanted pregnancy, only a double failure can cause an unwelcome conception.

Preventing unwanted pregnancy is always a joint responsibility. Both you and your partner would suffer adverse consequences. So you share the obligation to keep each other out of trouble. But the two sexes play different roles and suffer a different set of problems from this drama. Therefore, the information and advice that follows comes in two related, but divergent varieties. You may feel that you know much of this already, but in the heat of passion, some of your classmates will surely forget to their later regret. Read this chapter to help you be among those who always remember.

Men's responsibilities:

First of all, treat your girlfriend with kindness and consideration. You want that from her, and she deserves it from you. Follow the Golden Rule.

If a woman becomes pregnant, she gets to decide whether to have the baby or not. She can ignore your wishes completely.

After years of sex education, you know about STDs and should obviously take prudent precautions to minimize your chances of contracting any of them. You also need to take care of avoiding pregnancy. You can engage in a variety of pleasurable activities that present no risk of conception. If a relationship does progress to intercourse, always use a condom.

If a woman becomes pregnant, she gets to decide whether to have the baby or not. She can ignore your wishes completely and still hold you responsible for child support for the next eighteen years. The last moment the decision is in your hands is when you can still put on a condom. Girls forget to take birth-control pills by accident or accidentally on purpose. A diaphragm may fit improperly or be positioned incorrectly. No matter how it happens, if your girlfriend gets pregnant, you may be trapped into premature, involuntary fatherhood. The knock on your door in the middle of the night could be the process server delivering the paternity suit demanding eighteen years of your money for child support.

Conversely, if you decide you want the woman to have the baby, but she doesn't want to become a mother, you still have no say. She has the right to abort against your wishes, just as she has the right to carry a pregnancy to term and make you a father against your will.

You can prevent pregnancy, not with 100 percent certainty, but with reasonable assurance, by using a condom—every time. Every time means every time. No exceptions for birthdays, football victory celebrations, or the Fourth of July—even if your girlfriend insists that she has taken care of contraception. With bad luck, one omission can result in pregnancy (or an STD).

Women's responsibilities:

First of all, treat your boyfriend with kindness and consideration. You want that from him, and he deserves no less from you. Remember the Golden Rule.

Unless you desire all the changes a pregnancy will cause in your life, you must take charge of contraception.

The next thing to remember is that you can restrict sexual intimacy to a variety of pleasurable activities short of intercourse, and thereby avoid pregnancy altogether. You may want to keep in mind that conception and fetal development takes place entirely in your body, not your partner's. You're the one who gets pregnant.

If you decide to have an abortion, you're the one who goes to the operating room, receives medication, suffers pain, and bleeds to end the pregnancy. In addition to the physical pain, the whole process understandably causes emotional distress.

If you choose to carry the baby to term, it's your body that undergoes profound changes for nine months, labors through delivery, and needs to recover its shape. If you decide to give the baby up for adoption, you may have to overcome the emotional pain of separation. If you opt to keep the baby, you become responsible for a helpless new life. Motherhood is intensely time-consuming and takes a great deal of energy. If you want to complete college, pregnancy can most certainly derail your plans. An unplanned pregnancy from an uncommitted relationship that leads to single motherhood will interfere with your studies. Even when you have an exam the next morning, you can't ignore a colicky baby who keeps you up all night.

Unless you feel prepared for and desire all the changes a pregnancy will cause in your life, you must take charge of contraception. You cannot rely on your partner. He may forget about consequences in the heat of the moment. He may be ignorant, irresponsible, or simply relying on you to prevent pregnancy. By taking responsibility for contraception, you can avoid a lot of hassle and heartache.

When you both take precautions and look out for each other, you can enjoy a mutually pleasurable sexual relationship.

Points to Remember:

- Mutually satisfying sexual encounters need not involve intercourse.

- If your relationship does lead to intercourse, use a condom every time—even if you use other birth-control methods.

- Take responsibility for your actions. Don't rely on your partner to keep you out of trouble.

Part III

Beating Student Frustrations: Roll with the Punches

Years from now, you'll probably recall your college days as some of the best of your life. In the meantime, unprotected by the merciful haze of selective memory, your good experiences will have to coexist with stressful challenges and disappointments. In this section, we'll tackle and vaporize some potential sources of distress.

13

Avoid Boring Lecture Classes

A professor is one who talks in someone else's sleep.

—**W. H. Auden**
English poet/critic (1907-1973)

Professors advance their careers mainly through research and academic publications, not by their ability to teach. Except for the faculty teaching courses on the topic of education itself, your lecturers earned their doctorates in fields other than education—in different subjects that most likely intrigue them far more than teaching. Their employment contracts, however, require that they teach classes. Some like the idea and take pride in doing an outstanding job. They relish the opportunity to inspire students with a passion for their subjects (or at least with an understanding of why their subjects can inspire passion). Others merely go through the motions, regurgitating textbook material in a robotic monotone.

So, how can you avoid the latter group, the professors who could be marketed as a cure for insomnia? By doing some research before signing up for classes. For example, students at many universities publish guides that rate lecturers. Check out this resource if it's available at your school.

If you lose consciousness during a single lecture, you'll know that multiple class sessions could produce deep coma.

You can also query other students who have already taken a particular class. Unless your friends are looking for a good laugh at your expense by intentionally steering you in the wrong direction, you should get reliable reports on what to expect.

In an academic term prior to your enrolling in a class, audit a lecture to check out both the teacher and the subject. If you lose consciousness during a single sampling, you'll know that multiple sessions could produce deep coma.

Obviously, this research will become easier after you arrive on campus. So the greatest risk of enrolling in a snoozefest conducted by a mystery professor comes during your first term. Do whatever advance research you can. You might be able to consult friends who are already on campus. Perhaps obtain a faculty-rating guide by mail or over the Internet. Once you've done all you can, pray for good fortune.

Now, suppose you don't receive a positive response to your prayers and find yourself in Dr. Barry Boring's lecture hall. You're not totally out of options. You might be able to drop the class and enroll in another one. If you're taking enough other credits, you could also drop Boring and just carry a lighter schedule.

If you're stuck in the course for the term, you still have some additional options. At most universities, class attendance is not mandatory, especially in auditorium-sized lecture halls. Your grade may be based entirely on how you perform on exams and assignments. If the lectures provide little education, then you miss out on little education by being absent. You may be better off studying the material on your own.

You might be able to purchase class notes from a formal note-taking service.

To ensure that you don't miss crucial information, you have several choices. You can team up with a couple of classmates, and each of you can take turns attending lectures and sharing notes with the others. Alternatively, you might be able to purchase class notes from a formal note-taking service. Enterprising students at some universities earn money by attending lectures, taking comprehensive notes, and selling them to colleagues who either missed the class or feel that they could benefit from looking at a set of well-written notes. If this service is available for the Boring lectures, it may be a wise investment.

Some lectures and class announcements may be on the Internet. You might be able to get everything you need via your computer without ever attending a Boring class again.

Sometimes during your college career, you have no choice. You have to enroll in a mandatory course that only Dr. Snoozemore teaches. Here again, you have the options I've just described.

Please remember that this advice applies only to lectures that produce more yawns than education. I am certainly not advocating wholesale hooky—far from it. Students who cut classes miss out on a most vital element of college education.

And skipping labs, seminars, tutorials, or any other sessions that require active participation will count against your grades. So this information pertains to a miniscule fraction of all courses. In my four years as an undergrad, I only suffered through two classes that fell into this category.

With some research and a little luck, you could do even better than that. Don't neglect checking out courses and professors before registering for classes. The small effort involved will be amply rewarded by a far better-quality education.

Seek out star teachers.

Particularly for electives, where you have a choice of a variety of subjects, pick the class with the best professor. Seek out star teachers. They can inspire and entertain while they educate. Their classes are worth attending, whether you need the credits or not. If such a class doesn't fit into your course schedule, consider auditing sessions of it for fun instead of credit.

Teaching assistants can also make or break a course experience. As graduate students with recently acquired expertise in their fields, TAs often convey more passion for their subjects and put more effort into their teaching than many a jaded professor. TAs can clarify difficult areas, guide you to the important points and answer your questions. Of course, the quality of teaching from TAs varies as widely as it does among professors. If you have the opportunity, audit the first sessions of several TAs for a given class, then choose the best one.

Incomprehensible international instructors pose a related problem, but I most certainly don't mean every professor or TA with a foreign accent. So long as you can clearly understand them, your foreign-born teachers can deliver some of your most informative and inspirational lessons. So, don't be too quick to shy away from them. The reward for just a little bit of extra effort to get used to an unfamiliar accent could be an outstanding educational experience. Every large campus in America features superstar teachers who hail from other countries. But if an instructor's "English" can be understood only by people who speak his native language—if deciphering his idiom poses a greater challenge than mastering the course material—then opt out by using all the techniques enumerated earlier to avoid boring teachers.

While this chapter focuses on avoiding and coping with lousy lecturers, please remember that lectures need not be dull. They can entertain, inform, and even inspire. Well-known professors who consistently packed large lecture halls include Carl Sagan in astronomy, Joseph Campbell in literature, Richard Feynman in physics, and Indiana Jones in anthropology. (Okay, the last one performed in movie theaters instead of classrooms, but the first three were real-life professors.) Your campus, no doubt, features similarly fascinating teachers. So, please don't approach lecture halls with a negative attitude. With a little planning and the right mind-set, you can enjoy many great lectures during the course of your college education.

Points to Remember:

- Do research on professors before signing up for their classes.

- Pay attention to the quality of TAs as well as professors.

- Seek outstanding teachers.

14

Overcome Bad Exam Grades

It ain't over till it's over.

—Yogi Berra
(his second at bat in this book, see Chapter 8)

Despite your best efforts—or perhaps because of a temporary lack of effort—you might perform poorly on an exam and get a lousy grade. Bummer. So, what do you do next? Turn it around, of course.

Use the disappointment of a bad exam grade as motivation to start studying that day to turn things around.

You need to start studying that day to catch up to the level of knowledge you should have had when taking the exam in the first place. Begin *that same day* because disappointment can be a powerful motivator, and you don't want to lose that extra oomph. First, learn what you should have known for the exam. Then continue to move forward by mastering the new material. Get ready to ace the next exam.

Sometimes you can get fooled. A class that initially seems easy may suddenly become much more difficult. You might discover this just as you're studying for a midterm. Here, once again, the pre-deadline deadline can save your butt. By preparing for an exam early, you secure a cushion, a padding of additional time to learn material that turns out to be unexpectedly difficult.

Some classes offer a back-door way of improving your grade—extra credit. You earn it by doing some work beyond the basic requirements. Writing an additional paper or participating in a project may be a way of making up for a less-than-stellar result on an exam. Of course, it's extra work, but undoing a bad exam always takes more work than doing well in the first place.

Remember, no class is over till it's over. Never give up on a grade until after you've finished answering the last question on the final.

Let's take the issue of dealing with a sub-par performance one step further: suppose you get a grade below your expectations in a course. A bigger bummer, but not the end of the world. A single bad grade, even a couple of them, won't ruin your entire record. Not many graduate college with a 4.0. You do, however, need to show an overall pattern of good grades, especially in the courses considered most difficult. So long as you ace the bulk of your harder classes, your academic record will help you when applying for graduate school or a job.

Points to Remember:

- If you get a poor exam grade, start studying that day to improve your destiny.

- You can sometimes compensate for a low exam grade by doing extra-credit assignments.

- Remember: "It ain't over till it's over."

PART IV

Thriving: Make the Most of Your Experience

Still with me so far? Congratulations. We've covered the hard, the bad, and most of the ugly. It's now time to discuss some good stuff—fun, parties, and a few final points on how to make the most of college.

15

Wait Before You Leap: Fraternities and Sororities

I don't want to belong to any club that will accept me as a member.

—**Groucho Marx**
American actor/comedian (1890-1977)

Don't pledge at the start of your freshman year.

Of course, go to rush parties! Take advantage of free refreshments, cool music, lively entertainment, and the chance to meet some fellow students to hang with later.

Just don't pledge at the start of your freshman year.

It's too early. You don't know enough to make such a commitment. You don't know enough about the role and reputation of Greeks on campus, nor about the reputation of the particular house that's bidding you to join.

The role fraternities and sororities play in the social life on campus varies widely from one college to the next. In many

schools, only a small portion of students, fewer than five percent, join the Greek system. On some campuses, the *Animal
House* reputation of frat boys makes it harder, rather than easier, to get dates. At other schools, being a Greek carries a distinct social advantage. Even on those campuses, however,
some fraternities and sororities have poor reputations.

Your perspective on all this is bound to be less informed
when you first arrive on campus than it will be some months
later. Start attending classes, get a feel for the social scene on
campus, see how much time you could or would want to
devote to Greek activities. You can decide later whether you
want to join.

Saddling yourself with pledge duties while you're adjusting to college life is an extra burden you don't need.

Don't let yourself get pressured into pledging. Don't
believe that the invitation is made on a "now or never" basis. If
the guys or gals want you to join, they will let you do so the
following year. If they don't, perhaps they didn't think so
highly of you in the first place, and you'd be better off at
another house.

Pledging requires a significant time commitment. Saddling
yourself with pledge duties while you're adjusting to college
life is an extra burden you don't need. Fraternity or sorority
obligations can eat into your study time when you can least
afford it.

So, explore the Greek system. Attend all the parties you
want. Rock to their music. But in the end, dance to the tune

of your own best interests. Hold off on the decision to pledge until your sophomore year.

Points to Remember:

- Learn about the role of Greeks in the social life of your campus and about the reputations of the houses.

- Hold off on the decision to pledge a sorority or fraternity until your sophomore year.

16

Have Fun

If it's not fun, you're not doing it right.

—**Bob Basso**
American author/motivational speaker (born 1938)

I hesitate to say this. You're already an expert on this subject and will find abundant opportunities for terrific extracurricular activities on campus. The crucial point here is balance. Have a good time, but remember that you're in college to advance your education and earn a degree. *Classes always come first.* They won't, however, take up all your time. You not only can, but *absolutely should* take advantage of the many other pleasures of the university environment.

A significant part of your education will come from immersion in the campus environment.

Pick up the campus newspaper before your first class every morning and do a quick check for any announcements of interest. Perhaps a famous writer, artist, or politician will give a talk at noon. A musician may try out new tunes at a free concert. You could learn about a rally for the football team, a movie preview with the director present to answer questions, or a slide show about an international study program. A significant part of your education—and even more of the pure joy of being a college student—will come from university culture, an environment infused with vibrant and varied diversions.

If you participate in a program like intramural soccer or write for the campus newspaper, you establish a comfortable niche for yourself. You find a place you can hang out, a place where everybody knows your name, an environment conducive to forming strong friendships.

Don't hesitate to try new activities. Attend lectures by visiting speakers. Go to football games and gymnastics meets. Sample a broad range of cultural events—ethnic dance performances, foreign films, improvisational comedy shows. Take the opportunity to easily expand your horizons. You might discover a new passion—or several new passions.

Party hearty—an unnecessary reminder, I am sure. Just remember that you need to allocate enough hours to study and sleep. With good time management, you can enjoy everything college life has to offer while getting a great education.

Points to Remember:

- While classes always come first, feel free to take advantage of extracurricular activities.

- You'll have easy access to a broad range of diversions.

- Extra-curricular activities provide wonderful opportunities for expanding your horizons and for having a great time.

17

Take Pride in Your School

(ra ra sis boom ba...)
So be true to your school.

—**Brian Wilson** (of the Beach Boys)
American singer/songwriter (born 1942)

Look for positives in your environment.

Whether you attend the university of your dreams or the only college that stooped to admit you, you should take pride in your school. No matter which college you attend, the brightest students on your campus can compete with the smartest people anywhere in the world. The faculty of your school almost certainly includes outstanding teachers and scholars. The library contains more books than any human being can possibly read, and provides high-speed access to all the data on the Internet. More today than ever before, students everywhere can access campus resources to retrieve information from distant universities, libraries, and other sources of knowledge. Opportunities for a first-class education are all around you. Many graduates of your college went on to or will go on to distinguished careers and significant accomplishments. The education available to you at your school can be a stepping stone on your path to a brilliant future. Look for positives in your environment. It will make you happier, more content, and more proud of yourself. Be true to your school.

Points to Remember:

- No matter which college you attend, you have the opportunity to obtain a first-class education.

- Be proud of your college.

18

Be Grateful

Gratitude is not only the greatest of all virtues, but the parent of all the others.

—**Cicero**
Roman statesman/orator (106-43 BCE)

If you can be grateful for the opportunities and pleasures in your life, you will be happier and more successful. Attitude shapes destiny. No matter what's going on in your life, you can always find people who are better off, one way or another. Someone else may have higher grades, greater athletic ability, finer social poise, more beauty, greater wealth, or something else superior to what you possess. Don't lose sight of the fact that many others will be worse off in all those categories than you. As a college student in the United States in the twenty-first century, you have privileges and opportunities that most people in the world can only dream about. So, be grateful for what you have. Appreciate your good luck.

Grateful people are happy people.

Of course, it's okay—indeed both natural and desirable—to want more. You need to strive to achieve, and wanting more will motivate you to work toward your goals. Realize, however, that you have plenty already, and appreciate it. Grateful people are happy people. And happiness is contagious. So you owe it both to yourself and to those around you to be grateful for your good fortune. Remember this when something goes wrong in your life. Actually, you don't need to wait for anything to go wrong. Remembering how fortunate you are is a habit that will serve you well anytime. It can give you silent satisfaction, bring a smile to your face, and let you live as a happier person.

Points to Remember:

- Attitude shapes destiny.

- Gratitude leads to greater happiness and success.

- You owe it both to yourself and those around you to be thankful for your good fortune.

19

Be Kind

If you can't be kind, at least have the decency to be vague.

—Anonymous

Kindness begets kindness.

You're going to meet a wide variety of people over the next four years. Some will be nerdy, others socially poised. Many will struggle to make the grade, others will graduate with much less effort. Some will be clumsy, others natural athletes.

Whenever you come across colleagues lacking in some way, you can add to their misery by making fun of their shortcomings. Or you can be the good guy who comes to their aid, helps them out at an opportune time, and makes life better for a fellow student. Kindness begets kindness. The nerd you help out today can be in a position to return the favor later on. So, err on the side of thoughtfulness and compassion. You will feel better for it and so will the people around you.

Points to Remember:

- You have the power to make life easier for people you come across.

- Err on the side of kindness.

20

Remember Your Old Support System

You just call on me brother if you need a friend.
We all need somebody to lean on.

—Bill Withers
American singer/songwriter (born 1938)

The people who loved you last year still do. They remain as close as a telephone call or an e-mail. They miss you. They still want to be part of your life. They will be there for you when you need encouragement, advice, assistance, or a good kick in the butt. You can always reach out to any of them when you need help, when you're lonely, or just to stay connected.

Take the initiative and make the call yourself.

Your support system could include your parents, teachers, coaches, or high school friends. Don't hesitate to consult the people who love you, whenever the thought enters your mind. Don't wait for them to call you, especially when you need a supportive voice to lift your spirits. Take the initiative and make those calls yourself. The people at the other end of the line will be happy to hear from you.

Points to Remember:

- Stay connected to the people who care about you.

- They can provide timely support and encouragement.

21

Parting Advice: Recommencement

Teachers open the door, but you must enter yourself.
—**Chinese Proverb**

By going to college, you can look forward to many benefits including:

- **Education:** Acquiring knowledge that will help you throughout the rest of your life.

- **A degree:** Obtaining a diploma that will facilitate your path to a more interesting, fulfilling, and lucrative career.

- **Personal growth:** Taking part in experiences that lead to greater maturity and lasting friendships.

Graduating from high school is a major milestone, a turning-point in your life. As a college freshman, you now get to start anew, with a clean slate. It's an exciting moment, bursting with anticipation and hope. Take the habits that have produced success for you so far, and combine them with the advice in this book. Together, they can create a blueprint for transforming your next four years into a gratifying, memorable, and joyful experience.

That's it—except for these final comments.

Congratulations on all your achievements in high school.

Good luck! Learn a lot—both inside and outside the classroom. Have a blast!

978-1-60528-013-4
1-60528-013-5

Made in the USA